Pattie McCarthy's *extraordinary tides* gorgeously breathes the back and forth of water and liminal space but also racks serious balls. Bishop's verse that says where the land meets the sea is "literature"—here this idea finds a brittle, punctuated alphabet made of the things collected: oyster comma, gentle cloud commas. Simultaneously, McCarthy sees the world through the maintenance and survival of her own body, a witch's circle, and from her observations can build entire days, and entire beings: "We hold a useless language on our tongues, and it becomes useful." —Cynthia Arrieu-King, author of *The Betweens*

Tides churn, birds gyre, twilight turns to night and back to day. "It's the end of the world but / which world," these poems ask, pointing to all that cycles back. *extraordinary tides* attends to the "smallest stop in the relentless / present tense," to motion and stasis, to change and continuation. At the edge of the sea, holes in socks, salt in hair, these poems "write the paragraph of our place // again and again."
—Sarah Dowling, author of *Entering Sappho*

I was first drawn to Pattie McCarthy's *extraordinary tides* by the beauty and strangeness of its language. Strange compound words (some neologisms, some not) such as "wrackline," "boyfull," "holdfast," "distelfink," "bladderwrack," and "seastruck" seem temporarily agglomerated like the kelp and shells mixed in the latest high tide's wrackline. This book is a study of flux in the shape of sea and sky. It does as Lorine Niedecker recommended: It throws "objects to the flood." Not carelessly or nonchalantly. An object, an amalgam, is, "what makes a pause—even/the smallest stop in the relentless//present tense." There is a "we" in these poems that tries to puzzle out shapes and distinctions—"holdfasts." We keep track of the neap tides as well as of lent and yule in the Advent calendar. "We can tell a hawk from a heronshow." But still things slide—even the most important things:

the ocean took

the form of my daughter

& held her up

& held her up

the ocean took the form of

my daughter— a cormorant

It is the tension between tenuous solidity and flood that makes this work so beautiful and moving. —Rae Armantrout, judge for the Omnidawn Poetry Chapbook Contest; author of, most recently, *Conjure*

Pattie McCarthy brings the waterfront into our lexicon, asking the literary to kiss the littoral, where the archaic is made present, and the present is made historic when channeled through her vigilant ear and euphonic voice. In poems written at the wrackline—the vein where the ocean tongues the land—& in a time when the world thrashed and foamed in quarantine, McCarthy's coastal almanac helps us imagine what of the sea resists being bought and sold as a boardwalk sensation (then) and Instagram documentation (now). "tradition says clams are common property & the flats unleasable" writes McCarthy, in characteristically buoyant, full-throated verses of beguiling calm and razor-brisk wit. Reading extraordinary tides in these extraordinary times (to which Old English denotation the title hearkens), I am better anchored to observe what remains common amongst the species at the shore who insist that we can, still, "eke the ebb of it." If the tides are the intercessional prayers that sustain a cosmological love between the

moon and our planet, then McCarthy becomes, in this book, the trusty
translator of those abiding novenas. —Divya Victor, author of *CURB*

PREVIOUS BOOKS

Wifthing (Apogee Press, 2021)

Quiet Book (Apogee Press, 2016)

Nulls (Horse Less Press, 2014)

Marybones (Apogee Press, 2012)

Table Alphabetical of Hard Words (Apogee Press, 2010)

Verso (Apogee Press, 2004)

bk of (H)rs (Apogee Press 2001)

extraordinary tides

Cover art by Kate Kern Mundie, Fog (Belfast), 2019, oil on panel, private collection, and courtesy of the artist, www.katekernmundie.com

Cover design by Laura Joakimson
Interior design by Laura Joakimson
Interior typeface: Cochin and Didot

Library of Congress Cataloging-in-Publication Data

Names: McCarthy, Pattie, author.
Title: Extraordinary tides / Patricia Mary Frances McCarthy.
Description: Oakland, California : Omnidawn Publishing, 2023. | Summary: "extraordinary tides attempts to hold a position in the intertidal, the in-between place of not-quite-land and not-quite-sea. The poems engage time and tide, and our efforts to predict and know both. If the ground beneath us is always in flux, how do we know where we are? Considering the language of the tides, the poems in this chapbook make a wrackline palimpsest, a seastruck archive, a marginalia of the littoral"-- Provided by publisher.

Identifiers: LCCN 2023019297 | ISBN 9781632431172 (trade paperback)
Subjects: LCGFT: Poetry.
Classification: LCC PS3563.C3373365 E98 2023 | DDC 811/.54--dc23/eng/20230525
LC record available at https://lccn.loc.gov/2023019297

Published by Omnidawn Publishing, Oakland, California
www.omnidawn.com
10 9 8 7 6 5 4 3 2 1
ISBN: 978-1-63243-117-2

extraordinary tides

Pattie McCarthy

OMNIDAWN PUBLISHING
OAKLAND, CALIFORNIA
2023

contents

neap tide— autumn

the tidal forest is the whole
present tense— the first

winter full
moon in october

gossamer overcast
the wind catches— one

tree & then the next—
a tide that reaches the sky—

a desire path— a split
infinitive— intertidal fricative

form is content — content is form — it is the only commandment
but there is no shape to days

the long border of an evening intertidal
never resolves itself never dissolves

never solves for any variable —
it is simply stretched beyond recognition

or usefulness — a king of nothing
& nowhere — but if we want

process not product — which we do — then
it will be evening all season & we will stretch into it

the whelked & jinxed intertidal
furbelows seaweed —

a boat neaped — you've got to be
kidding me   I say five times a day

waved like the enridged sea —
if I could take the sound of you into

my mouth   I would
work double tides —

on the impossibility of measuring the coastline [1]
shorter stretches of evening — a quarantine

how language inhabits a line that moves [2]
fishhawks & distelfinks — a littoral

zone — the middle intertidal & its predatory
snails — its rockweed & mud

why go anywhere alone —
the summer tide shed into a crackle

the clean corner of this room in view
low water & a singular good tiding

eke the ebb of it — the sound of traffic
not the sea

wrackline palimpsest
I am so pure I am a bore

when dusk shed its x
& waved across both

the sea & middle
english & will arrive today

precisely at 5.00 p.m.
& have the least

difference between high
& low & sea & sky & light

May - November 2020

[untitled yule tide]

on the east coast in winter   above or below the tide-line
one walks in water or in mud   there is no dry land [3]

clam holes in mud
& sand— why not

look to that like the sky—
winter fishery

tradition says clams are common property
& the flats unleasable—

birds try & fail to gyre— at least
for a while— the middle of the water is a window

the sky spangled with crows
a night body of water

serrated wrack   saw wrack   toothed wrack
dulse spiraled tidy into

a whole universe [4]— bladderwrack
is a cunt in the granite —

textured uncertain driftlines
things aren't always so

conscientious as to draw
their soft edges for us

we move singularly like
a liquid — soft shallows

what if instead of horizon
lines we read low

drain tides   boats soft aground   the middle
littoral sugar kelp woven — I will never have

enough I say to your
sleeping inscrutable shape

snow on snow   snow
on snow   fallow waves

find your V   goose
whirl the fuck up

warm winter windows
ladybugs on them

oyster comma
oyster ear

half a conch crown
clam fan light

my oldest hears sounds that I
cannot — including the sky

the sky keeps bright
eyes on us — we

look up into the cold
the tide makes

a friction like
a song in glass

that is   the tide sings
while it spins in glass [5]

so deep midwinter the light turns iron
there is no end to your tongue

at this time of a winter's day one can see
the light turn & begin to flake & burn [6]

& while it's a turn I always notice
something far away changes key

there is no perfect
line except the wrackline

which is infallible
it's too cold to do

anything complicated
come to bed   come to bed   come to bed

in marginalia season —
hawkless salt-hag

the tide adds or subtracts
a causeway — a lightening

line between the deeper
blues & though I

look with adoration at these
lines for hours

nothing comes
back to me

seastruck grid of skies
a whole year— more

skies than days [7]
in five days I saw

at least sixty skies —
gray wool—broken orange

glass—burning—oystershell—
gray cool—boyfull—clearing blue—

mirror calm—gentle cloud commas—
whirled up storm waves—

a calendar of salt & tides
& birds scything the full sky

it took me so long to write this
it's over — but that's

the way with everything we
say in unison with briny

tongues— tide me
over — if you put

something in a circle —   no one
will want to cross it

I don't even know what's good
anymore— I only know

what makes a pause— even
the smallest stop in the relentless

present tense —
wery ɗo water to wore

weary aɗ water on the ɗhore [8] —
the ocean told us

how we felt & who
were we to argue

—December 2020 - March 2021

lent — in extraordinary tide

I am not giving anything up
I am already a saint —

having given up
most of what one gives up

we have all the marks of winter
on our bodies — we become saints

when we are too old for what if —
we write the paragraph of our place

again & again — I am
a bird on the border of what

we become saints through
a total lack of privacy — we find

everything in need of a mend —
I watch my breath

drift to the street — our hands
scorched through holes in the potholders —

I am judgmental of drive-through ashes —
I earn my ashes

the old-fashioned way — with bad habits —
we can tell a raven from a crow

I am so pure I am a monster
I am 'finding the masterpiece mystery inspector attractive' years old

I am 'complaining about the clocks' years old
I am 'buying high arch insoles for my doc martens' years old

I am 'leave your socks on — it's cold' years old
I am 'watching masterpiece mystery online illegally' years old

I am 'teaching students how to cite a tweet in MLA' years old
I am 'enjoying a song by the cure in the grocery store' years old

I am 'watching brexit in bed' years old
I am so pure I am a bore

our children shout in suburban
late winter twilight — we cover

the maps with traffic
we put our feet through

our socks & our fingers through
our towels & we know that

saints do not require privacy—
our books — our eyes — need better light

it's the end of the world but
which world

our flesh is tested in crabbed lent
we buy chincoteague salties for five dollars

a dozen on the roadside
we note the crocuses burst up

while we were at work
we can tell a swift from a swallow

we searched for hagstones & found
none in the wrackline of wicked march

we hold a useless language on our
tongues & it becomes useful

longer stretches of evening & stiff
contagious fiddlehead curl

our whole long-legged 1970s is in every
photo of you as a child — we know

there's nothing better to do
I am the flutter that's

left in the nest
your kitsch is on fire — the squirrels

rummage at this time — our sundust
I am so pure & so lonely — please come home

I went in a building only
to look at how the light entered it

I was taking all the people
out of my poems — I've let them

back into the poems
I am in a starbucks — exhausted

I am going to let that text buzz again
we can tell a hawk from a heronshaw

we find it unsurprising that sainthood is boring —
winter misfit mother

we're in the yellow I've
dreamt about — shaped by tracery

a pinch & stitch
instead of a cervix — a bloodless

pinch — I do feel
the space of it filling in

rooting for the hawk as crows
drive her from the cemetery

across the street — rooting for
the hawk in hawk v pigeon

the lifelists of saints —
our hawks drag

the smoked sky behind them —
our heronshaws drag

the wading sky behind them —
our crows drag

the blossom sky behind them —
our grackles drag

the long-legged sky behind them —
our finches quietly drag the oystershell sky behind them —

the lifelists of saints feature
mostly ordinary backyard birds

we indulge in cloud discourse
lententide as a sheltering-in

the hedge all flutter
I am a saint in your mouth

we are an uncountable noun
we know the only

way poets take revenge is to make
work for themselves

—Lent 2019, Lent 2020

neap tide — spring

the middles english & littoral give up
their exes   their wrack   their holdfasts

their shelter feathers — put that
howl in my mouth

slow soft dazzle
there is nothing but

relentlessness — when the water takes
the foreshore   the birds move up

the rocks — the fizzle of waves over
pebbles & shingle

the ocean took the form of a curlew —
sorry   a cormorant —

the ocean took
the form of my daughter

& held her up
& held her up

the ocean took the form of
my daughter —   a cormorant

& held her up
& held her up

ghosts of salt & frost on the rocks —
which word for *hole*

we'll use depends upon
the lobster's intent [9] —

my son — his sunshine
halo well salted — sifts

pebbles shingle shells spirals   & tells
me a pebble is 4 to 6.4 centimeters across

on the complicated relationship
between wrack & rack — see usage note

& I have been inland a while
the virgin of the dry tree

the tidal shift is not
seamless — even

the neaps mark
circatidal margins

whelks fast during neap cycles
unknot the fishing rope to unrestrain

the wind— we were quizzed on the birds
we made flashcards of all the trees

what if an old wife is what
is necessary to predict the weather

dried sugar kelp can predict the weather
for example — the rocks here winter

woven with it — crenulated — what if
an oyster allows you to safely swallow the sea

whole — *a word like* hair *comes*
tangled with associations with seaweed & swimming[10] —   & held her up

the tender point of mean high water
held her up   & held her up

January - April 2021

notes

[1] artist Mary Frances, *isolated spaces XLVII*, title of photograph from 9 May 2020 / https://twitter.com/maryfrancesness/status/1259170689648594947

[2] Danielle Vogel, *Edges & Fray*

[3] J.A. Baker, *The Peregrine*, "December 3rd"

[4] after the work with seaweed by Jeannet Leendertse

[5] after Luke Jerram's acoustic installation / sculpture *Tide*

[6] J.A. Baker, *The Peregrine*, "December 21st"

[7] after Mary Burger's *Skies of 2020*

[8] *wery so water to wore* is from the Harley Lyric beginning "Betwene Mersh and Averil"; the translation here is Eleanor Parker's

[9] I owe this to the opening of Manchán Magan's book *Thirty-two Words for Field*

[10] Nicholas Allen, *Ireland, Literature, & the Coast: Seatangled*, page 207

acknowledgements

"lent— in extraordinary tide" first appeared in periodicities, ed. rob mclennan. "neap tide— spring" first appeared in On The Seawall, ed. Ron Slate.

[untitled yule tide] first appeared in APARTMENT, eds. Jack Snyder, Marietta Pasotini, & Michael Joseph Walsh.

Thank you to these editors for their support.

Pattie McCarthy is the author of seven books of poetry, most recently *wifthing*. A former Pew Fellow, she teaches literature and creative writing at Temple University, where she is a non-tenure track professor..

extraordinary tides

by Pattie McCarthy

Cover art by Kate Kern Mundie

Cover design by Laura Joakimson
Interior design by Laura Joakimson

Cover typeface: Didot
Interior typeface: Cochin and Didot

Printed in the United States
by Books International, Dulles, Virginia

Publication of this book was made possible in part by gifts from Katherine
& John Gravendyk in honor of Hillary Gravendyk, Francesca Bell, Mary
Mackey, and The New Place Fund

Omnidawn Publishing Oakland, California

Staff and Volunteers, Spring 2023

Rusty Morrison senior editor & co-publisher
Laura Joakimson, executive director and co-publisher
Rob Hendricks, poetry & fiction editor, & post-pub marketing
Jason Bayani, poetry editor
Anthony Cody, poetry editor
Liza Flum, poetry editor
Kimberly Reyes, poetry editor
Sharon Zetter, poetry editor & bookdesigner
Jeffrey Kingman, copy editor
Jennifer Metsker, marketing assistant
Sophia Carr, marketing assistant
Katie Tomzynski, marketing assistant